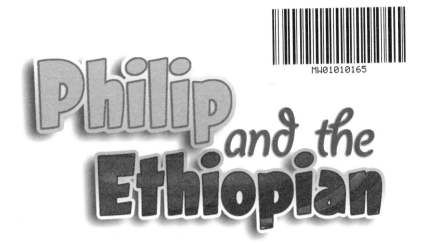

Philip and the Ethiopian

Acts 8:26–40 for children

Written by Martha Streufert Jander
Illustrated by Kathy Mitter

Arch® Books
Copyright © 1996, 2004 Concordia Publishing House
3558 S. Jefferson Avenue, St. Louis, MO 63118-3968

Along a dry and dusty road
A chariot bumped and swayed.
The man who rode that desert trail
Had come a long, long way.

His home was Ethiopia,
Where Candace ruled the land.
He was in charge of all her wealth—
A most important man.

He'd been in great Jerusalem
To worship God, most high.
Now he was trav'ling home again
Beneath the bright blue sky.

He read the Bible as he rode,
But then a frown appeared;
For while he knew the words he read,
Their meaning was not clear.

Meantime, upon another road,
A man named Philip walked.
He served his Savior, Jesus Christ,
Of Him he always talked.

The Spirit spoke to Philip then.
He said to him, "Now go!
Stay near the chariot that you find
Along the desert road."

So Philip found the puzzled man,
And called out as he ran,
"How much of what you're reading do
You really understand?"

"Slow down and stop!" the man called out.
His driver pulled the reins.
Then as he turned to Philip, said,
"Come, sit here, and explain."

"Who is the One that's talked about?
Who's like a sheep that's led—
And like a lamb that makes no sound?"
The man, confused, now said.

So Philip joyfully explained,
"My Jesus was the one
Isaiah long ago foretold—
God's one and only Son.

"He came to earth to live for us,
To die for all our sin.
But three days after that He rose
From death to life again."

The wheels kept rolling them along
Beneath the desert sky.
The man told Philip, "I believe
That Jesus came to die.

"I do believe He died for me
To take my sin away.
Look! There is water near," he cried,
"Baptize me without delay."

"Slow down and stop," he called again.
They started on their way,
And walked down to the pool below,
Where Philip stopped to say,

"I baptize you today, my friend,
In God, the Trinity,
In God the Father, God the Son,
And God the Spirit, three."

Out of the water, dripping wet,
Came Philip and the man.
They praised the Lord! They sang for joy!
Back to the road they ran.

Without a blink, without a sound,
The Spirit of the Lord
Now carried Philip far away
To tell of Christ adored.

And like the man that Philip met,
We too go on our way,
We praise the Lord because we're His,
And we serve Him every day.

Through God's own Son, Lord Jesus Christ,
Our every sin's forgiven,
And because of Him, one day we'll be
With God, at home in heaven.

Dear Parents:

The story of Philip and the Ethiopian is a delightful one to discuss with your child. Notice the firm guidance the Holy Spirit gives Philip in his witnessing. In Acts 8:29 we read, "The Spirit told Philip. 'Go to that chariot and stay near it.'" Take a moment to pray for the Spirit's guidance in your family's witnessing. Help your child think of friends and relatives with whom you can share the Good News about Jesus. Talk about the sudden way the Spirit took Philip away (Acts 8:39). Explain to your child that God also puts us in the right spot at the right time to witness for Him.

Tell your child that the Ethiopian treasurer was reading a scroll that contained only the Old Testament. He did not know the Lamb whom Isaiah prophesied would silently and unjustly die for our sins. Role-play a witnessing situation. Let your child tell you how Jesus died on the cross and rose again so we may have forgiveness and eternal life.

Compare the Ethiopian man's Baptism with your child's. Look at your child's Baptism certificate and pictures taken on that day. Rejoice together in the new life God gives us through water and His Word.

The Editor